The Connector's Code

Building Bridges through Powerful Communication

Table of Contents

Chapter 1. Introduction

Welcome to our special report on "The Connector's Code: Building Bridges through Powerful Communication." Delve into the invigorating world of effective communication as we unpack groundbreaking insights and strategies designed to transform mere dialogue into lasting bridges of understanding and connection. This isn't just a hub of theoretical knowledge; it's a wellspring of actionable wisdom that's sure to make you a veritable maestro in the symphony of communication. Whether you are a leader seeking to motivate, an employee aiming to collaborate better, or simply an individual yearning to forge deeper personal relationships, this special report is your ticket to a profound communicative awakening. So, let's flip the pages and start the journey because the power of words waits for no one, and the world is ready for your message, clearly and compellingly delivered!

Chapter 2. The Power of Words: Redefining Communication

Words, deep and profound, form the cornerstone of our existence and the beacon guiding our journey of connection and comprehension. Life's mysteries unravel themselves in conversations, and the strength of words unfurls its might in our efforts to build bridges and transcend borders. A profound exploration of the potency of words, their appropriate application, and their role in reshaping effective communication awaits you - a journey promising discovery and edification.

2.1. The Essence of Words

Words, in their unique quintessence, are more than mere strings of vowels and consonants. They are thoughts encapsulated into a tangible form, evolving from the abstract domain of cognition to the tangible realm of expression. From French philosopher René Descartes' "Cogito, ergo sum" (I think, therefore I am), it can be inferred that our very existence gets validated through the process of thinking, and words enable us to extend our thoughts from individual cognition to collective consciousness.

The power of words can be felt in the compassionate consolation of a friend, the burning intensity of a lover's confession, or the rousing speech of a leader. In essence, words have the power to heal, invigorate, provoke, and inspire, and they pave the path for genuine human connections.

2.2. Driving Words with Intent

Honing the power of words isn't merely about possessing an elaborate vocabulary; it's rooted in sharpening intent and refining thought processes. Hence, let's lay some groundwork. Consider the three Rs: Reason, Reflection, and Responsiveness. These can guide you in molding effective dialogue.

Reason – The key to powerful communication resides in understanding your own motivations while expressing yourself. Is your intention to persuade, inform, or question? Recognizing your purpose can bring clarity in choosing the right words.

Reflection – Reflecting upon the impact of our words can help us build empathy, allowing us to convey our message more compassionately.

Responsiveness – Adaptability in communication is essential. By being responsive to the listener's inputs, we demonstrate respect for their point of view and foster more engaging and effective conversations.

2.3. The Art of Listening

Communication is a two-way process. The ability to listen actively proves as powerful as the skill of articulating thoughts. The Greek philosopher, Epictetus, once said, "We have two ears and one mouth, so we should listen more than we say." In an effective communication process, understanding the speaker's intent holds as much weight as conveying your own message.

To harness the true potential of words, it's crucial to pay attention to others, hear between the lines, decode underlying messages, and develop a reciprocal conversation. Through listening, we validate others' thoughts and feelings, fostering a climate of mutual respect and understanding, further reinforcing the very foundations of communication.

2.4. Cultivating Emotional Intelligence

The power of words transcends the boundaries of intellect and ventures into the realm of emotional intelligence. Empathy, self-awareness, and emotional control emerge as significant aspects of optimizing our communication.

Empathy – Words can bridge the gap between hearts when laced with empathy. Understanding others' perspectives can help in choosing words that resonate and inspire connection.

Self-awareness – Knowledge of one's emotional state and its influence on one's communication style makes for more genuine, relatable exchanges.

Emotional control – While expressing oneself, managing one's emotions is key. Emotions serve to add color to our words, but they mustn't cloud our communication, transforming it into impulsiveness.

2.5. Mastering Non-verbal Communication

As powerful as words are, they often come accompanied by an invisible orchestra of non-verbal cues like gestures, postures, eye contact and more, amplifying, explaining or sometimes contradicting the verbal messages. A firm handshake, a warm smile, or an enthusiastic nod, all heighten the impact of words. Hence, mastering non-verbal communication is as crucial as selecting the right words for successful connections.

In conclusion, words, in their profound and multifaceted might, lead the charge in the quest for effective communication. By imbuing words with intent, cultivating the art of active listening, embracing emotional intelligence, and mastering non-verbal cues, we create a symphony of communication that sings to the tune of understanding, empathy, and connection. As we delve deeper into the powerful world of communication, let's remember: Words cast shadows and light alike. It's in our power to ensure they illuminate rather than obscure, resonate rather than alienate, and connect rather than divide.

Chapter 3. The Role of Empathy in Effective Interactions

In the tableau of human interaction, empathy stands out as a pivotal element around which our connections revolve. A simple, often overlooked tool, empathy has the profound capacity to engender understanding, foster collaboration, and ultimately bridge the gaps between us.

3.1. Empathy: A Vital Ingredient of Communication

Empathy—the ability to temporarily step into someone's shoes, to view the world from their perspective—provides the antidote to misunderstanding. In this realm, our unique perspectives unfold into a shared narrative, devoid of the isolating walls of ego.

Understand that empathy doesn't necessitate agreeing with the other person's viewpoint. It entails embracing a curious eagerness to explore, comprehend and validate their emotions and experiences. This shift in perspective paves a path strewn with shared understanding, trust, and mutual appreciation, the cornerstones to fruitful communication.

3.2. The Science of Empathy

Empathy is woven into the very fibre of our humanity. According to research, specific regions in our brain such as the anterior insula and the anterior cingulate cortex activate when we put ourselves in another's shoes. In fact, these neuronal responses mirror those elicited when we experience emotions ourselves. Consequently, we're not only bound by unifying narratives or language, but also by the invisible ties of a shared biological response. This concerted neurochemical dance underscores our capacity to empathize, to resonate emotionally with others, which forms the bedrock of effective interactions.

3.3. Unpacking the Types of Empathy

Deepening our understanding of empathy requires differentiating between its types—cognitive empathy, emotional empathy, and compassionate empathy.

Cognitive empathy, or perspective-taking, relates to our intellectual ability to perceive and understand others' emotions without necessarily sharing them. For instance, we might comprehend that a colleague is distressed over a project deadline without feeling their despair.

Emotional empathy, also called affective empathy, deals with vicariously sharing and experiencing another's emotions. Here, seeing a friend in tears could evoke a similar emotional reaction in you. This shared emotional experience often leads to an immediate, embodied understanding of the person's emotional state.

Lastly, compassionate empathy—harmonious unity of cognitive and emotional empathy—propels us to take action. It motivates us not just to understand and share others' emotions, but to remedy their distress.

3.4. Harnessing Empathy for Effective Interactions

Adopting an empathetic lens profoundly transforms our interactions. Instead of viewing conversations as transactional exchanges, we begin to perceive them as opportunities for mutual growth and connection. As we step beyond the confines of our preconceived notions and assumptions, our connections deepen, trust grows, and dialogues become more meaningful and productive.

In conflict resolution, empathy plays an indispensable role. It enables us to understand the underlying emotions, positions, and interests of conflicting parties which affords us an insightful platform to engage constructively.

In the workplace, empathetic leaders build stronger, more resilient teams. They navigate the delicate balance between achieving organizational goals and being understanding of their team members' circumstances.

On a personal level, empathy builds bridges of connection, transforming ordinary interactions into extraordinary bonds of understanding, solidarity, and mutual respect.

3.5. Empathy: The Pathway to Influence

When you demonstrate authentic empathy towards others, they're more likely to reciprocate by trusting and revealing their authentic selves to you. In other words, by creating an environment of psychological safety—where people feel valued, heard and not judged—you increase your ability to influence.

Powerful influencers from politics to business have recognized this secret to their success. Deeply understanding and connecting with their audience not only allowed them to resonate with their message, but also to inspire action.

3.6. Cultivating Empathy

Empathy isn't an inherited trait; rather, it's a skill that can be nurtured and developed. Here are a few strategies for cultivating empathy:

1. Active Listening: This means fully focusing on the speaker, avoiding interruptions, and responding thoughtfully.

2. Open-mindedness: Resist quick judgments and be open to different perspectives.

3. Empathetic language: Use language that shows understanding and acknowledgment of the other person's feelings.

4. Observing Non-verbal cues: Pay attention to body language, facial expressions, and other non-verbal cues that can shed light on the speaker's emotional state.

5. Practice Mindfulness: Being present allows you to engage deeply in the conversation and build a stronger connection with the speaker.

The capacity to cultivate empathy within ourselves stretches far beyond fostering meaningful connections—it is a pathway towards becoming better, more compassionate human beings. As we augment our ability to empathize, we not only bolster our communication skills, but we also contribute more positively to our society—a society that understands, values, and respects its diverse constituents.

Empathy—the capacity to understand and share others' feelings—is a mighty tool. It bridges the gap between misunderstanding and understanding, high-handedness and respect, isolation and connection. Nestled within this tool, lies the power to transform mere transactions of dialogues into enriching exchanges of human understanding. So as you step forward in your communicative journey, remember to pack empathy in your toolbox. Its transformative power awaits your discovery.

Chapter 4. Active Listening: The Forgotten Component

Active listening is a concept that underpins effective communication and forms the bedrock of all meaningful relationships. Despite its critical nature, our everyday communication practices barely offer it the importance it deserves. Introspect for a moment and ask yourself: Are we truly lending an ear to those speaking to us, or are we just mechanically running our minds on autopilot, offering pre-rehearsed responses?

It's time to realize that listening doesn't equate to simply staying silent while others talk. On the contrary, it's an active process that demands full attention and engagement. As we dive deeper into active listening, you'll discover its various facets, understand its enormous benefits, and acquire strategies to become a seasoned active listener.

4.1. The Mechanics of Active Listening

Let's first dissect what active listening truly constitutes. It's the process of attentively hearing, comprehending, evaluating, and then responding to a speaker. Rather than passively 'hearing,' active listening is about 'understanding' the spoken words in real-time, underlining key points, clarifying information, and offering a thoughtful response. It's like being a detective, paying attention not only to the spoken words but also to the unspoken cues, thus drawing a complete picture.

The mechanics of active listening involve three key steps:

1.**Comprehension**: It is the initial process of understanding the speaker's words, fundamentally decoding the received message.

2.**Retention**: This step involves remembering the key discussion points. It helps in both immediate response and future recollection of the interaction.

3.**Response**: A critical component of active listening as it completes the communication loop. It involves verbal or non-verbal feedback to the speaker, confirming that the message was effectively understood.

4.2. Active Listening versus Passive Listening

People often confuse passive listening with active listening. Passive listening is similar to hearing - sounds are simply entering your ear, but might not be interpreted or even remembered.

Consider watching a movie while browsing on your phone. You're aware of the dialogues and even react to dramatic scenes – that's passive listening. But, if asked to recall specific dialogues or narrate the storyline, you might struggle. Passive listening disseminates information, but with no guarantee of retention or comprehension.

On the flip side, suppose you are attending a business meeting or a counseling session. You'd be fully engaged, interpreting the ideas, understanding unspoken sentiments, responding appropriately – that's active listening. It's participatory in nature, cultivates understanding, and aids in constructing meaningful replies.

4.3. The Art of Being Present

Active listening begins with being present in the moment. We live in a world defined by multi-tasking, where we are physically present in one place, mentally in another. To genuinely hear and understand someone, we need to break free from this shackle.

In active listening, each conversation is a lucid lake, not a turbulent ocean shared with other cognitive operations. We need to halt our cognitive traffic, provide undivided attention to the speaker, and truly immerse ourselves in the dialogue.

Being present also involves regulating our emotions. With the hustles of life, we often carry a tint of sentiments, ranging from anger to sorrow, which can bias our listening. It's essential to counterbalance these emotions, bringing a clean slate to every conversation.

4.4. Non-Verbal Signals: Reading Between the Lines

Active listening covers the whole landscape of communication, not just the audible words. Over 90% of our communication is determined by non-verbal cues such as gestures, postures, facial expressions, and even the pace of speech. As an active listener, one must sharpen the radar of their perception to detect these signals.

Maybe it's the reassuring nod from your colleague that she agrees with the presented idea, the frown from a friend that hints that he's not thrilled by what you're saying, or the furtive glance from a speaker signaling their discomfort. Non-verbal cues are a speaker's unsaid words that whisper crucial insights.

4.5. Empathetic Responding: The Final Seal

The response a listener provides can either open doors for further communication or bolt them shut. An empathetic response, demonstrating understanding and respect for the speaker's perspectives, fosters conducive communication.

Instead of formulating your response while the speaker is still talking, listen to understand. Once they finish, summarize the points to confirm your understanding and then offer your viewpoint. Avoid being judgmental or providing solutions unless asked for. Let the response be a bridge, not a barricade.

Active listening in a nutshell is not an acquired skill. Instead, it's about rewiring our mindset, being present in every conversation, and making an emphatic effort to understand others. Whether it's your colleague, your boss, or the check-out cashier at the local supermarket, each one has a story waiting to be told. All they need is an active listener. Are you ready to be one?

Remember, in the symphony of communication, the best musicians are not just those who play their notes with passion but those who listen keenly to the notes played by others. So tune your ears to the melody of your speaker's words and get ready to create harmonious compositions.

Chapter 5. Non-Verbal Cues: The Silent Language

The most vital and often overlooked part of communication is conducted without uttering a single word. Non-verbal cues, such as body language, facial expressions, and gestures, tell volumes about what we think, feel, and intend. A raised eyebrow, a folded hand, or a straightforward gaze: each of these could reveal what countless words might fail to express.

5.1. Understanding Non-Verbal Communication

Non-verbal communication is a complex yet fascinating dimension of human interaction that extends beyond mere body movements. It encompasses various elements, ranging from our physical appearance and voice modulations to timing, space, and touch. Delving deeper, we'll explore each component.

5.2. Physical Appearance

Initial impressions are hugely influenced by physical appearance. The way we dress, groom, and carry ourselves hold significant cues about our personality, mood, profession, and socioeconomic status.

For instance, the difference between an individual in a tailored suit and aboard room demeanor versus someone in casual clothes and a relaxed posture is immediate and evident, spanning conclusions about their respective professions or the gravity of the situations they are in. Also, cultural differences play a key role in the interpretation of physical appearance and should not be neglected.

5.3. Vocal Element

Often tagged under 'paralanguage,' the vocal aspect of non-verbal communication involves aspects like pitch, rate, volume, and voice quality. Together they can add new layers of meaning to the words being spoken.

The same phrase, pronounced with various voice modulations, can have dramatically different interpretations. A low, slow "I understand," may be seen as empathetic, while a fast, high-pitched "I understand," might come across as sarcastic or dismissive.

5.4. Body Movement and Posture

This aspect of non-verbal communication is the most observed and discussed. It covers a wide array of elements, such as movements, gestures, and overall body stance – generally categorized as 'kinesics.' Your standing or sitting stance says much about your comfort, confidence, and openness in a situation; while gestures, such as the way you use your hands while talking or your facial expression in response to information, can reflect your true feelings and thoughts.

5.5. Eye Contact

Managing eye contact can be one of the most potent tools in the realm of non-verbal communication. In most cultures, maintaining steady eye contact indicates trustworthiness, attentiveness, and engagement, while avoiding it may hint at the opposite. However, extended eye contact can sometimes backfire and lead to discomfort or be perceived as hostile.

5.6. Spatial Dimension: Proxemics

Proxemics is the use and perception of one's physical space. An individual's use of space, distance maintained in communication, or physical territory at home or the workplace can deliver powerful messages about power dynamics, territoriality, intimacy levels, and individual preferences.

5.7. Role of Touch: Haptics

From a reassuring pat on the back to an assertive handshake, touch is potent in expressing feelings. In professional settings, it's used sparingly and purposefully. In personal relationships, it's more intimate and comforting, emphasizing the multiplicity and complexity of haptics.

5.8. Non-Verbal Cues: A Cultural Perspective

Non-verbal cues are heavily influenced by one's cultural background, and what seems appropriate in one culture may be considered offensive in another. Therefore, understanding cultural variance in non-verbal cues is crucial for frictionless cross-cultural communication.

5.9. Decoding Non-Verbal Cues

Decoding non-verbal cues is no less than deciphering a dynamic, in-the-moment puzzle. Every gesture, posture, eye movement, and vocal intonation can have varying interpretations based on the context, the individuals involved, and their cultural background. Yet, by building our awareness and understanding of these cues, we can significantly enhance our communicative proficiency.

5.10. Applications of Non-Verbal Communication

In realms like professional negotiations, personal relationships, or diplomatic interactions, understanding non-verbal cues can be a game-changer. Reading between the lines, sensing the unsaid, and understanding the underlying emotions or intentions can help create an atmosphere of trust, cooperation, and empathy.

So, the unspoken, the silent, the subtle – the realm of non-verbal cues—holds potent insight into our shared human experience. The more we understand these subtle signals, the better we can bridge the communication gap, fostering connections that resonate on deeper, more empathetic levels.

In essence, by harnessing the power of non-verbal cues in our interactions, we graduate from being mere participants in the conversation to skilled composers in the symphony of communication, sparking dialogues that resonate, inspire, and connect.

Chapter 6. Constructing Positive Dialogues: The Art of Framing Ideas

The construction of positive dialogues lies at the heart of effective communication. It springs forth from an amalgamation of careful idea framing, adept listener understanding, and strategic verbal channeling.

6.1. Crafting Your Message

The manner in which we design our message plays a crucial role in how it is received. Disclose your thoughts in a concise, clear, and coherent manner. This reflects respect for the listener's time and understanding abilities and sets a constructive tone for the dialogue. Always anchor your messages in truth, even when tackling sensitive topics. Honesty reinforces trust and keeps the dialogue free from manipulative undertones.

Another key aspect involves anticipating reactions. Identify potential points of contention upfront and address them immediately in the dialogue. Doing so establishes openness, maintains the constructive tone, and preempts misunderstanding.

Lastly, balance both informative and persuasive communication. While it's vital to present facts and data logically, it's equally important to weave in a persuasive element that compels action or agreement. To this end, consider using metaphors or analogies, which can make complex ideas more relatable and convincing.

6.2. The Power of Positivity

A positive orientation gives your dialogue its ideal ambience. Affirmation and optimism are infectious – they facilitate rapport-building and foster an environment that encourages open dialogue. Express positivity through appreciative language. Applaud your listeners' achievements, skills, and ideas. Affirmative expressions such as 'good point', 'I agree', or 'that sounds useful' helps validate them and pave the way for reciprocal positivity.

However, positivity should not result in avoidance of disagreement or critical feedback. It's about turning negatives into constructive criticisms that enhance the dialogue's overall value. This approach binds conversations with nobility and resolve, and it leaves no room for destructive negativity, making dialogues more positive and productive.

6.3. Reflective Listening: The Parallel Dialogue

Reflective listening emphasizes reiterating the speaker's messages in your own words to ensure understanding. It's a powerful tool in building bridges across significant gaps in perception, value systems, or backgrounds. This mechanism offers two key benefits: it reassures the speaker that they've been understood, and it allows you to confirm your comprehension of their message.

Employ phrases such as 'What I'm understanding is...', or 'If I understand you correctly...' to operationalize reflective listening. Reflective listening fosters empathy and patience, ingesting the conversational rhythm with understanding and respect.

6.4. Nonverbal Communication: The Silent Dialogue

In face-to-face dialogues, nonverbal cues comprise roughly 55% of the message, even overtaking verbal content. Hence, mastering this unspoken language accentuates your communicative prowess.

Pay attention to body language, facial expressions, eye contact, and postural nuances. Maintain an open posture to project receptivity. Regular eye contact exhibits focus and honesty. Mirroring your partner's nonverbal signals shows empathy and creates rapport. Be aware of cultural diversities that may influence interpretations of nonverbal cues. Non-verbal eloquence shapes the dialogue's accompanying melody, lending it rhythm, pace, and depth.

6.5. Closing the Dialogue: The Lasting Impression

Dialogues are like stories; they need fulfilling closures. Summarize the salient points of the conversation to reaffirm understanding. Use this opportunity to clarify ambiguities and invite final thoughts from your dialogue partner. Express appreciation for their time and insights.

Concluding a dialogue on a positive, appreciative note reinforces the constructive ambience and leaves a lasting favorable impression. It bookmarks the conversation effectively and strengthens the bridge of understanding built through the dialogue.

In conclusion, constructing positive dialogues is an artful interplay of idea crafting, positivity, listening skills, nonverbal communication, and satisfying closure. It requires continuous conscious effort and practice. Yet the payoff, in terms of resultant effective communication and thriving relationships, is well worth the input.

Communication is indeed a bridge, and the effectiveness of its construction hinges on the architect – the communicator. Let's bring our energies together and build bridges that are not only sturdy, but also offer a delightful crossing experience.

Chapter 7. Overcoming Barriers in the Bridge of Communication

The bridge of communication, like any physical bridge, is plagued by potential barriers which, if not properly addressed, can lead to ineffective communication or, worse, complete communication breakdown. From sharpening our listening skills to developing a deep understanding of our audience, from taking into account cultural diversities to embracing digital advancements, this chapter offers a granular exploration on how to deftly overcome these barriers to forge a strong, reliable bridge of communication.

7.1. The Importance of Listening

Listening isn't merely an act of receiving sound; it's an art entailing interpretation, understanding, and response. The failure to listen actively poses a significant barrier to effective communication. Active listening requires full engagement, a process that demands time and patience. We miss vital information when we only hear the words but not the context and emotion enveloping them.

First, ensure that you're focusing fully on the speaker. Avoid environmental distractions like the buzzing of a phone or notifications on a computer. Second, provide feedback through verbal or non-verbal cues, such as paraphrasing the received message to validate your understanding or nodding to signal involvement.

7.2. Communication and Cultural Diversity

In our increasingly globalized world, we often interact with people from various cultural backgrounds. Misinterpretations stem from cultural nuances, whether they are verbal, non-verbal, or societal. A phrase that is perfectly acceptable in one culture might be offensive in another. It's essential to respect and understand these cultural differences to prevent them from becoming barriers to effective communication.

- Learn about different cultures: Educate yourself about the cultures of your peers and embed this awareness into your communication.

- Embrace diversity: Acknowledge individual experiences as uniquely important, even if they deviate from yours. This mindset builds bridges, respect, and mutual understanding.

- Promote Inclusivity: Cultivate an inclusive environment that places value on open dialogue and different perspectives.

7.3. Non-Verbal Communication

Non-verbal communication often conveys more than spoken words. Body language, facial expressions, gestures, and even the tone of voice can influence the effectiveness of our communication. Misinterpreting these cues can cause miscommunication.

To foster effective non-verbal communication: - Mind your body language: Stand or sit erect to demonstrate confidence and openness. - Maintain steady eye contact: This signals attentiveness and respect towards the speaker. - Adjust your tone: Match your verbal content to project sincerity and trustworthiness.

7.4. The Digital Factor

As technology evolves, so does the way we communicate. Digital tools provide diverse channels to communicate faster and more efficiently, but they can also become a barrier if they're not tailored to fit the message or the user's skillset.

For digital communication to be successful: - Choose the right platform: Understand the strengths of different platforms, then decide which best suits the content and context of your message. - Be concise and clear: Digital communication often benefits from succinctness. Avoid overly complex jargon or exceedingly long sentences. - Promote digital literacy: Encourage and support your peers in improving their digital skills and understanding different platforms.

7.5. Impediments of Emotion and Bias

Emotion and bias inherently affect communication. They can distort our perspective, influence our interpretations of messages, and even lead to conflicts. It is crucial to identify and manage these emotional and biased responses to promote unbiased communication.

To conquer these impediments: - Develop emotional intelligence: Learn to understand, use, and manage your own emotions in positive ways to communicate effectively. - Practice Self-awareness: Reflect on your predispositions and prejudices, and consider how these impact your communication. - Encourage openness and trust: Breeding a culture of openness creates an environment conducive to honest and meaningful conversation.

In conclusion, overcoming barriers in the bridge of communication isn't a one-time task, but a continuous process that demands conscious effort, willpower, and adaptability. By employing these strategies, you are well-poised to build a solid bridge, one where powerful communication flows unhindered, fostering understanding, connection, and collaboration. Understanding that communication isn't solely about speaking, but rather about connecting and embracing the many subtleties of human interaction, is your first confident step towards that splendid bridge of communication.

Chapter 8. Cultural Differences in Communication: Breaking the Norms

In our interconnected world, the ability to communicate effectively across cultural lines is of paramount importance. It's not just about knowing the language of our interlocutor, but also understanding their customs, norms, worldviews, and communication styles. This chapter will dive into the intricate and fascinating world of cultural communication patterns, exploring their diversity, cracking their codes, and providing you with actionable insights to break the norms and pave your way to communication mastery.

8.1. Understanding Cultural Norms

Cultural norms are implicit, unwritten rules that govern behavior within a community or society. They are deeply ingrained within individuals from an early age, shaping their perceptions, attitudes, and reactions. Understanding these norms is akin to decoding a secret language—a language that is spoken through non-verbal cues, contextual clues, and subtle nuances.

In essence, when communicating across different cultures, it's crucial to recognize and respect these norms. The famous aphorism, "When in Rome, do as the Romans do," encapsulates the essence of this approach. Yet, it's also important to break these norms when necessary, in pursuit of clearer communication and mutual understanding.

8.2. Communication Patterns Across Cultures

Cultures differ in how they value direct and indirect communication. High-context cultures, such as many Asian cultures, rely heavily on implicit messages, requiring individuals to read between the lines. On the opposite spectrum, low-context cultures like the United States and many Western societies prefer explicit and direct communication.

While high-context communicators might find low-context methods blunt or lacking in tact, low-context communicators might find high-context methods obtuse and foggy. Recognizing these differences is integral to effective communication.

8.3. The Role of Nonverbal Cues

Beyond words, nonverbal cues play a pivotal role in cultural communication. These include facial expressions, gestures, touch, eye contact, personal space, and even silence. About 60-70% of communication is nonverbal, emphasizing the importance of understanding these cues for effective cross-cultural dialogue.

For example, in Northern Europe, maintaining a fair amount of personal space is respected, while in Latin cultures, closer proximity is seen as a signal of warmth and friendliness. Similarly, in some Asian cultures, direct eye contact can be considered disrespectful, while in most Western cultures, it's perceived as a sign of honesty and confidence.

8.4. The Power of Active Listening

Active listening is a powerful tool across all communication landscapes, but it becomes particularly crucial when navigating cross-cultural terrains. It involves fully focusing on the speaker, acknowledging their message, and offering feedback when necessary.

The key lies in understanding that active listening is not just about hearing the words that are being spoken; it's about comprehending the context, the emotion behind the words, and the unspoken elements of the conversation. It's this nuanced understanding that forms the bedrock of cross-cultural communication.

8.5. Breaking the Norms: When and How?

Respecting cultural norms is pivotal, yet breaking them might be necessary in some instances, especially when they serve as barriers to effective communication. The challenge lies in discerning when to adhere to the norms and when to push against them.

When norms perpetuate misunderstanding, enforcing stereotypical beliefs, or hindering clear communication, it may be time to break them. However, this must be done tactfully, with cultural sensitivity, empathy, and the clear intention of advancing mutual understanding.

In conclusion, effective cross-cultural communication is a delicate balance of understanding, respecting, and sometimes breaking cultural norms. It's a dance— one that requires patience, practice, and respect for your dance partner. As with any skill, mastery comes with time and effort. Embrace this journey and watch as horizons of understanding open before you.

Chapter 9. Conflict Resolution: Turning Tides through Talk

Conflict, an unwelcome yet inevitable guest in professional and personal relationships, often brings with it a host of challenges. Whether it's a small dispute between coworkers or a complex, multi-layered disagreement, conflict, if left unchecked, can undermine unity, productivity, and satisfaction. However, resolving these conflicts isn't about turning a blind eye or quelling the fire alone. It's about transforming the tides through dialogue, morphing the turbulence into a wave of understanding and mutual respect.

9.1. The Anatomy of Conflict

Understanding the anatomy of a conflict is imperative in any conflict resolution approach. Conflict usually entails opposing interests, where at least one party perceives a threat to their needs, interests, or concerns. It may reflect underlying needs and power dynamics, often shaped by our past experiences and human psychology.

Internally, conflict can lead to feelings of anger, fear, despair, and anxiety. Externally, it can manifest as a discordant situation that destabilizes the environment. However, at its core, conflict is a difference in perspectives that can be mitigated through constructive communication, acknowledging, and understanding the others' contexts.

9.2. The Power of Dialogue

At the frontmost line of conflict resolution, dialogue stands as a potent tool. Conversations geared towards resolution aim at understanding the other party's perspective, reaching consensus, or agreeing to disagree respectfully.

Prior to diving into the waters of dialogue-driven conflict resolution, it's essential to create an atmosphere that supports open and respectful communication. The parties need to be open to hearing and being heard, and everyone should have an equal opportunity to express their feelings and concerns.

The communication strategy should be geared towards a solution, focusing on the problem and not on the person. It is more about active listening, empathizing with the other person's situation, providing feedback, and suggesting actionable steps.

Dialogue can turn tides if it encapsulates the transactional model of communication, which suggests that both sender and receiver are equally responsible for the communication. It's not merely about expressing one's view but equally about tuning into the other's frequency, to find a common ground where both parties feel heard and understood.

9.3. Equipped with Empathy

There's an indispensable element in any dialogue-driven conflict resolution approach: empathy. The capacity to understand or feel what another person is experiencing from within their frame of reference helps in resolving conflict amicably. It's the personification of the saying, "walk a mile in someone else's shoes," which allows a deeper understanding of their standpoints.

Empathy-driven conversations emphasize shared goals over the differences. They help identify areas of common ground, enabling a shift from a competitive, win-lose outlook to a collaborative problem-solving stance. Quite symbolically, it turns the stage from a battleground to a meeting ground.

9.4. Principles of Dealing with Conflict

There are strategic principles designed to aid in managing conflicts through productive conversation:

1. Define the Dispute: Clearly define the nature of the conflict. Are you arguing about facts, methods, principles, or values?

2. Foster Trust: Build an atmosphere of trust. It helps open up dialogue and provides a safe space for parties involved to express their views.

3. Focus on Listening: Practice active listening. It's important to understand that listening involves not only hearing the words but also interpreting and understanding the message.

4. Practice Empathy: Develop and harness empathy. Empathy fuels connection, and connections often lead to more harmonious relationships.

5. Seek Solutions: Pay emphasis on exploring solutions. Move the conversation from a failure-focused to a future-oriented dialogue. Encourage parties to brainstorm ideas in order to find potential solutions.

6. Reframe Positively: Reframing is a powerful tool in conflict resolution. It involves restating negative statements into positive assertions, thereby promoting a solution-focused dialogue.

9.5. Making Amends through Mediation

Often, a mediator can help steer conflict towards a resolution. Mediators are trained to ensure that communication remains civil, constructive and focused on the goal. They help in reality-testing the assumptions, facilitating empathy and reframing the dialogue towards mutually agreed resolution. It's about retaining balance in situations where the subjective nature of the conflict can make impartiality complex.

In conclusion, turning tides through talk is more than a possibility; it's a proven strategy. Learning the art of transactional and empathy-driven communication can help build bridges, turning conflict situations into opportunities for growth and understanding. Like a well-conducted symphony, the mix of active listening, empathy-driven dialogue, and negotiation leads to harmony where dissonance once ruled. It's about making music where noise existed, echoing the power of words over the clatter of conflicts.

Take this knowledge, grasp the potential within every conversation, and begin turning the tides. After all, resolving conflict is not just about quieting storms, but about harnessing their energy and directing it towards a brighter peace. So gear up and tune in, because the dialogue of peace waits for no one, and the world is ready for harmony through your voice.

Chapter 10. Harnessing the Power of Digital Communication

As the 21st century unfolds, we stand at the cusp of a digital revolution that is constantly redefining how we communicate. Leveraging these digital tools can create a more effective and efficient communicative matrix, but their abundance can often be overwhelming. What tools should we prioritize? These first steps on our journey of exploration begin with a deep dive into the various tools at our disposal.

10.1. Understanding the Digital Landscape

Valuable digital communication is predicated on an understanding of the digital landscape. This means familiarizing yourself with the various platforms available today, from email and chat-based platforms to social media and virtual reality.

Before you leap into using these tools, it's important to figure out what each one does and how it can fit into your communication strategy. Indeed, various social media platforms have different uses; while Twitter might be great for short, snappy updates, LinkedIn would be your go-to for professional networking and outreach.

Consider chat-based platforms like Slack or Microsoft Teams. These platforms can be excellent for real-time, internal organisational communication. They're designed to be quick, informal, and immediate. They're perfect for a rapid-fire exchange of ideas, but may be less suited for nuanced, thoughtful conversations.

10.2. Email: The Digital Cornerstone

Email remains the cornerstone of digital communication in the professional realm even as new tools and platforms surface. Its broad adoption, cross-platform compatibility, and asynchronous nature make it unbeatably versatile and reliable.

But the omnipresence of email presents unique challenges. Our inboxes are inundated with a flurry of emails daily, which can easily lead to "email fatigue." The key, then, is to ensure your emails stand out from the crowd.

First and foremost, the subject line of an email is your first – and sometimes only – chance to grab your recipient's attention. A vague or apathetic subject line can often lead your email to be lost or disregarded entirely. Strive for a compelling and concise subject line that accurately reflects your email's content.

The content of your email should also reflect a respect for the reader's time and attention. Prioritize clarity and conciseness; an efficient executive summary at the top of your email allows for your message to be received effectively, whether or not the reader has time for the full text.

10.3. The Power of Social Media

Social media has become a crucial platform for organizations and individuals alike, providing a mechanism through which to reach a vast and diverse audience. Each social media platform is a different beast and knowing how to tame each one can lead to effective and successful communication.

Twitter, for instance, thrives on brevity. Its fast-paced nature means that maintaining relevance requires regular posting while being sure each tweet holds value. Facebook, on the other hand, does not require as much frequency but requires more depth in each post. LinkedIn is mostly a professional platform, and the posts are valuable as long as they add to your brand or work life.

Mastery over these platforms is not limited to understanding their dynamics but also involves thoughtful content creation. In a world where every individual and organization is vying for attention, unique, meaningful, and engaging content is key.

10.4. Virtual Conferencing: Bridging The Distance

Virtual conferencing tools like Zoom, Microsoft Teams, Google Meet, etc, have gained immense popularity, particularly in light of the current global situation. They serve as critical platforms for conducting virtual meetings, webinars, or even social gatherings.

The key to effective communication in these mediums is mastering the fine balance between tech etiquette and traditional meeting decorum. Keeping your camera on during a meeting to create a more personal touch, maintaining a clean and professional background, or using the mute button when not speaking are all part of this new-age etiquette.

To enhance understanding and optimize meeting time, using the chat box function to ask questions or share relevant information can be helpful. Polls or reactions available on some platforms can provide instant feedback without disturbing the meeting's ebb and flow.

With this detailed knowledge of the digital tools at our disposal coupled with a sophisticated command over traditional communication principles, one can navigate the new era of digital communication, leveraging it to build powerful bridges of understanding. There's a whole world of opportunities that await at your fingertips; make sure that every digit (pun absolutely intended!)

counts by using your digital tools to enhance and optimize your communication strategies. After all, the power of words amplified by technology is limitless.

The digital revolution has democratized information and communication like never before; ensuring we can make the most of it requires that we understand these tools, adapt to them, and ultimately harness them. This isn't just about keeping up with the times, but about taking the reins and forging our own digital paths towards effective, efficient, and powerful communication. The future of communication is here and now - and it's digital.

Your move!

Chapter 11. The Connector's Future: Evolving Communication in the 21st Century

In our journey through the vast realm of communication, we have discovered its fundamental role in connecting individuals, organizations, and societies at large. As we stand on the brink of a new era, it becomes imperative to understand how these connections will evolve in the future and what role we, as communication champions, would play in shaping this evolution. Let's dive deep into this exploration in the 21st century.

11.1. The Dawn of Digital Communication

The advent of digital technology has revolutionized the landscape of communication. Today, we are no longer restricted to face-to-face conversation or physical letters. Digital platforms enable us to communicate instantly with anyone, anywhere in the world.

Emerging technologies such as Artificial Intelligence (AI), Augmented Reality (AR), and Virtual Reality (VR) are reshaping communication norms. AI chatbots, for example, can simulate human language and make interactions more efficient. AR and VR can provide immersive communication experiences connecting people on a deeper level.

Despite these advancements, digital communication has its pitfalls too. The lack of physical cues and nuances that are intrinsic to in-person communication can distort the intended message and lead to misunderstandings. Therefore, building bridges in the digital world requires keen awareness of these challenges and the application of effective strategies to overcome them.

11.2. Humanizing Digital Interactions

As digital technology is becoming more prominent, humanizing digital interactions is crucial to maintaining empathic bonds. Communication must transcend beyond simple data transmission to emotion transmission. This not only involves understanding the emotional context of the message but also responding in a way that demonstrates empathy.

Personalized communication approaches, storytelling techniques, and Emotional Intelligence (EI) skills are paramount in achieving this. An essential strategy is to interpret digital cues accurately. For instance, tone, word choice, and the speed of response could signify a person's emotional state.

Also, digital etiquette rules – such as responding within an appropriate time and avoiding capital letters that may come off as shouting – are essential in crafting thoughtful digital interactions.

11.3. Adapting to Cross-cultural Communication

In today's globalized world, cross-cultural communication is an integral part of professional and personal life. Cultural intelligence and adaptability play a significant role in bridging communicative gaps and fostering mutual respect and understanding.

The ability to understand and respect diverse cultural norms, beliefs, and communication styles can prevent miscommunication and misunderstandings. Recognizing cultural differences in body language, communication context (high or low context), and courtesy norms are fundamental.

Also, exhibiting cultural sensitivity, such as acknowledging different religious practices or taboos, can create a respectful and inclusive communication environment.

11.4. Building Emotional Resilience for the Cyber Age

With the transformation of the communication landscape, emotional resilience is a must-have skill. Digital communicators must prepare themselves to face communication challenges such as cyberbullying, information overload, and digital exclusion.

Emotional resilience can help individuals navigate these challenges by helping them manage their emotions effectively in stressful situations, maintain positive communication, and adapt to change. Mindfulness practices and emotional regulation can significantly enhance one's emotional resilience.

11.5. Communication Ethics in the Digital World

Communication ethics form the bedrock of credible and trustworthy digital relationships. Honesty, transparency, confidentiality, and respect for one's digital data are embedding ethical practices in communication.

It goes beyond just avoiding falsehoods; it means acknowledging and rectifying errors in communication, preserving the confidentiality of sensitive information, and treating all individuals with respect online.

In conclusion, the evolving landscape of communication in the 21st century needs connectors to adapt and equip themselves with new skills and strategies. Yet, the core principle remains the same - treating every communication as an opportunity for creating human connections built on understanding, respect, and empathy. As communication evolves, so must we, preserving the essence of empathy and humanity in every interaction. As we move ahead, the future of communication seems challenging yet promising, with endless opportunities to build bridges and connect the world.